Have

A MEDIEVAL CHRISTMAS

!

Love,
Jerr
11/02

✠

The words are taken from the Tyndale translation of the Bible
from the Gospels of St Matthew and St Luke.

A MEDIEVAL
CHRISTMAS

A Bulfinch Press Book
little, brown and company
Boston • New York • Toronto • London

THE ANNUNCIATION

✠

AND IN THE SIXTH MONTH THE angel Gabriel was sent from God unto a city of Galilee, named Nazareth, to a virgin spoused to a man whose name was Joseph, of the house of David, and the virgin's name was Mary. And the angel went in unto her, and said: Hail full of grace, the Lord is with thee: blessed art thou among women.

When she saw him, she was abashed at his saying: and cast in her mind what manner of salutation that should be.

✠

THE ANNUNCIATION

AND THE ANGEL SAID UNTO HER: fear not Mary: for thou hast found grace with God. Lo: thou shalt conceive in thy womb, and shalt bear a son, and call his name Jesus. He shall be great, and be called the son of the highest. And the lord God shall give unto him the seat of his father David, and he shall reign over the house of Jacob, and of his kingdom shall be none end.

Then said Mary unto the angel: How shall this be, seeing I know not a man? And the angel answered and said unto her: The holy ghost shall come upon thee, and the power of the highest shall overshadow thee. Therefore also that holy thing which shall be born, shall be called the son of God. And behold thy cousin Elizabeth, she hath also conceived a son in her age. And this is her sixth month, though she be called barren: for with God can nothing be unpossible. And Mary said: behold the handmaiden of the lord, be it unto me even as thou hast said. And the angel departed from her.

THE VISITATION

✠

AND MARY AROSE IN THOSE DAYS, AND WENT into the mountains with haste, into a city of Jewry and entered into the house of Zachary, and saluted Elizabeth. And it fortuned, as Elizabeth heard the salutation of Mary, the babe sprang in her belly. And Elizabeth was filled with the holy ghost, and cried with a loud voice, and said: Blessed art thou among women, and blessed is the fruit of thy womb. And whence happeneth this to me, that the mother of my Lord should come to me? For lo, as soon as the voice of thy salutation sounded in mine ears, the babe sprang in my belly for joy. And blessed art thou that believedst: for those things shall be performed which were told thee from the Lord.

And Mary abode with her about a three months, and returned again to her own house.

THE NATIVITY

✠

AND IT CHANCED IN THOSE DAYS: there went out a commandment from August the Emperor, that all the world should be taxed. And every man went unto his own city to be taxed. And Joseph also ascended from Galilee, out of a city called Nazareth, into Jewry: unto the city of David which is called Bethlehem, because he was of the house and lineage of David, to be taxed with Mary his spoused wife which was with child.

And it fortuned while they were there, her time was come that she should be delivered. And she brought forth her first begotten son, and wrapped him in swaddling clothes, and laid him in a manger, because there was no room for them within in the inn.

DEVS IN

ens Adcunam.
in adintonium
meum intende.
Homne ad adinuandu

ANNUNCIATION TO THE SHEPHERDS

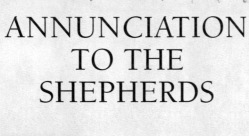

ND THERE WERE IN THE same region shepherds abiding in the field and watching their flock by night. And lo: the angel of the Lord stood hard by them, and the brightness of the Lord shone round about them, and they were sore afraid. But the angel said unto them: Be not afraid. For behold, unto you is born this day in the city of David, a saviour which is Christ the Lord.

And they came with haste, and found Mary and Joseph and the babe laid in a manger.

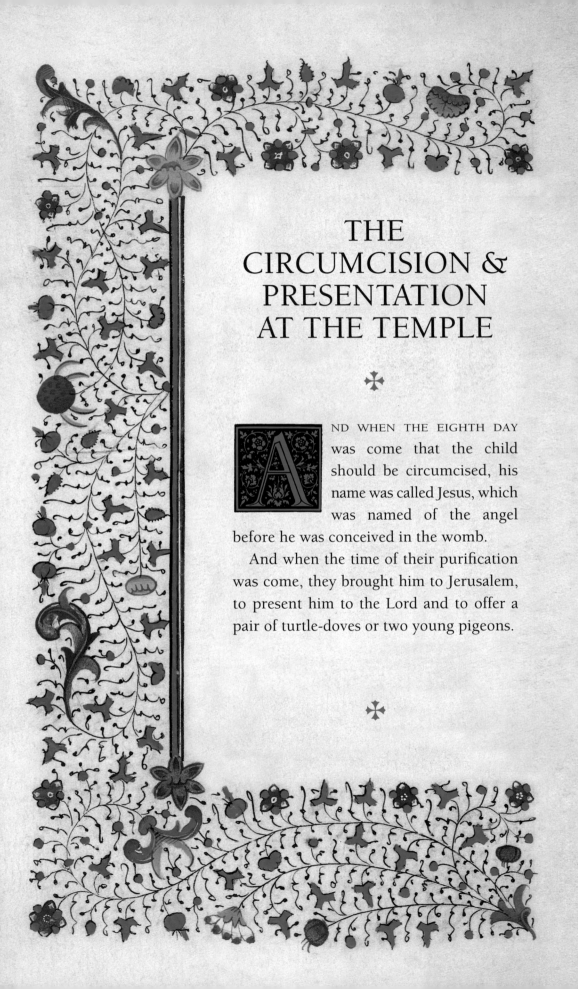

THE CIRCUMCISION & PRESENTATION AT THE TEMPLE

✠

AND WHEN THE EIGHTH DAY was come that the child should be circumcised, his name was called Jesus, which was named of the angel before he was conceived in the womb.

And when the time of their purification was come, they brought him to Jerusalem, to present him to the Lord and to offer a pair of turtle-doves or two young pigeons.

✠

eus ín adíutoꝛ
íum meum
ítende. omíne

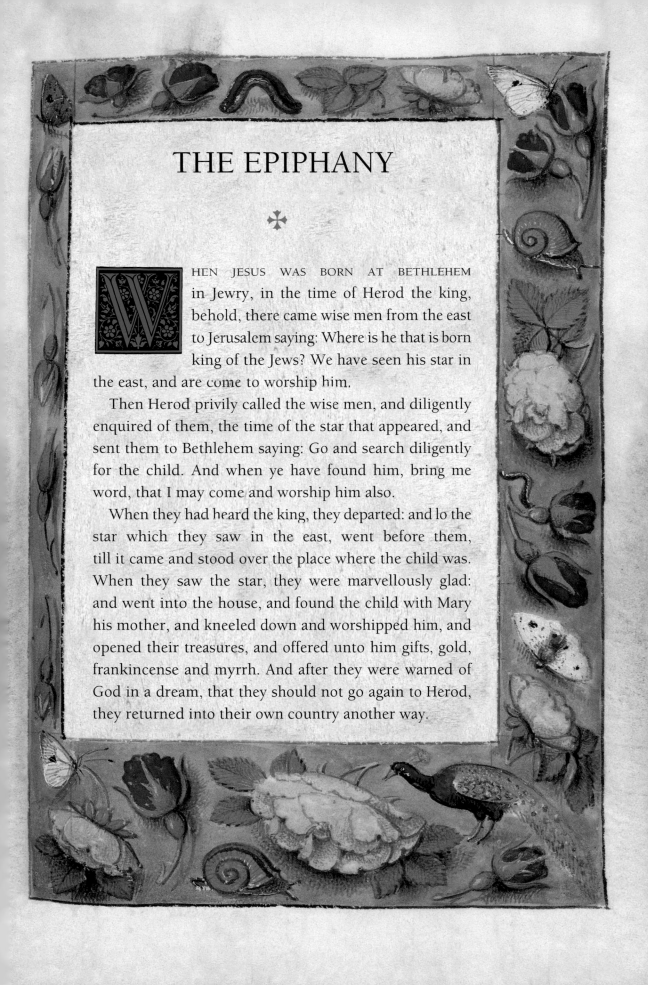

THE EPIPHANY

✙

WHEN JESUS WAS BORN AT BETHLEHEM in Jewry, in the time of Herod the king, behold, there came wise men from the east to Jerusalem saying: Where is he that is born king of the Jews? We have seen his star in the east, and are come to worship him.

Then Herod privily called the wise men, and diligently enquired of them, the time of the star that appeared, and sent them to Bethlehem saying: Go and search diligently for the child. And when ye have found him, bring me word, that I may come and worship him also.

When they had heard the king, they departed: and lo the star which they saw in the east, went before them, till it came and stood over the place where the child was. When they saw the star, they were marvellously glad: and went into the house, and found the child with Mary his mother, and kneeled down and worshipped him, and opened their treasures, and offered unto him gifts, gold, frankincense and myrrh. And after they were warned of God in a dream, that they should not go again to Herod, they returned into their own country another way.

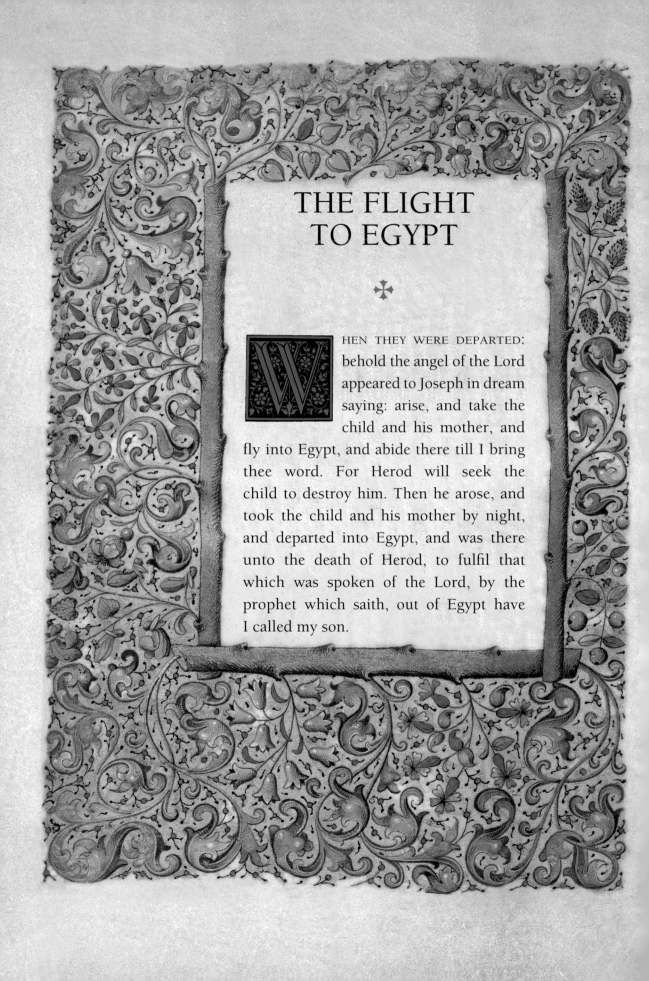

THE FLIGHT TO EGYPT

✠

WHEN THEY WERE DEPARTED: behold the angel of the Lord appeared to Joseph in dream saying: arise, and take the child and his mother, and fly into Egypt, and abide there till I bring thee word. For Herod will seek the child to destroy him. Then he arose, and took the child and his mother by night, and departed into Egypt, and was there unto the death of Herod, to fulfil that which was spoken of the Lord, by the prophet which saith, out of Egypt have I called my son.

Eus madiuto
rum meum
intende.

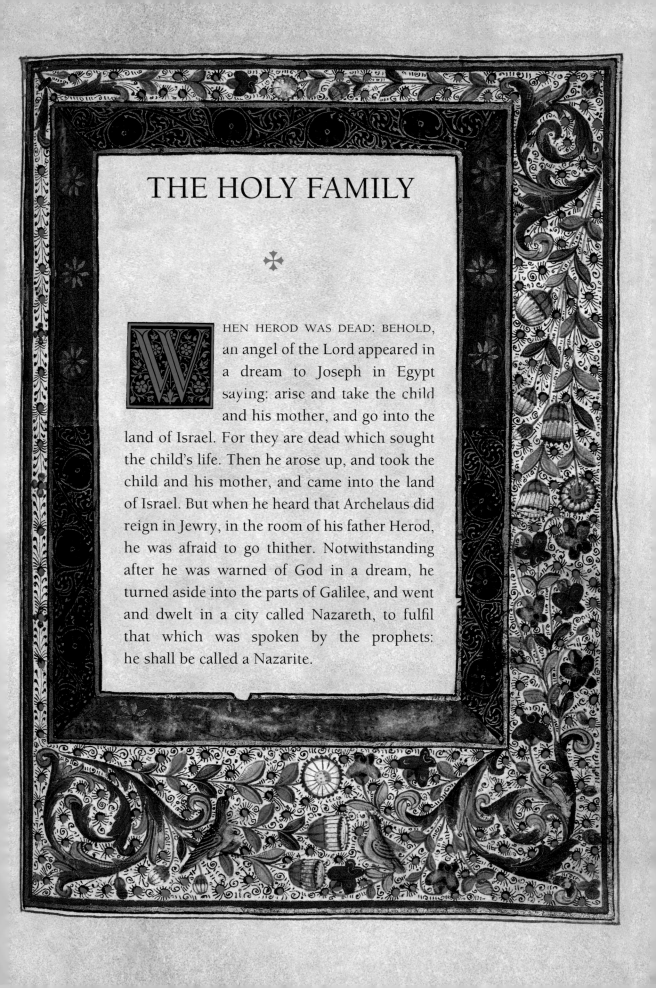

THE HOLY FAMILY

✠

WHEN HEROD WAS DEAD: BEHOLD, an angel of the Lord appeared in a dream to Joseph in Egypt saying: arise and take the child and his mother, and go into the land of Israel. For they are dead which sought the child's life. Then he arose up, and took the child and his mother, and came into the land of Israel. But when he heard that Archelaus did reign in Jewry, in the room of his father Herod, he was afraid to go thither. Notwithstanding after he was warned of God in a dream, he turned aside into the parts of Galilee, and went and dwelt in a city called Nazareth, to fulfil that which was spoken by the prophets: he shall be called a Nazarite.

(LEFT) *Front cover*

The Bedford Hours. BL Additional MS
18850 f.65. Paris, about 1423.
260 x 180 mm

THE BEDFORD HOURS, one of the
grandest illuminated manuscripts
ever produced, was originally owned by
John of Lancaster, Duke of Bedford and his
wife Anne of Burgundy, married in 1423.
On Christmas Eve 1430, the Duchess, with
her husband's approval, offered the Hours
as a gift to their nephew, nine year old
Henry VI, who was staying with them at
Rouen before his French coronation. The
marginal decoration of the manuscript is
unusually rich and original, comprising
over a thousand small, circular miniatures.

(RIGHT) *Page 7 (title page)*

Hours of Etienne Chevalier.
BL Additional MS 16997 f.21.
France, early 15th century.
160 x 115 mm

THIS EXQUISITE SMALL Book of Hours,
regarded as one of the artist's finest
works, was illuminated in the first quarter
of the 15th century by the Boucicaut
Master, a leading Parisian book painter of
the day. He is named in honour of his
principal patron, the Maréchal de
Boucicaut, who was taken prisoner at the
Battle of Agincourt and died in England
in 1421.

(LEFT) *Pages 8 - 9*

THE ANNUNCIATION

BL Additional MS 30899 f.1.
Paris, early 15th century.
200 x 140 mm

ONE OF SIX detached leaves from a
Book of Hours, typical of the best
contemporary Parisian illumination. The
delicate marginal decoration, along with
singing angels, includes a pair of putti
fencing with windmills. The arms of an
early owner have been painted out in the
lower margin.

(Right) *Pages 10 – 11*

THE ANNUNCIATION

The Hastings Hours. BL Additional MS
54782 f.73. Flemish, about 1480.
165 x 120 mm

THIS MANUSCRIPT was made for William,
Lord Hastings, a close friend of King
Edward IV. Hastings was beheaded in 1483
on the orders of the Duke of Gloucester,
afterwards King Richard III. Its delicate,
beautiful miniatures, surrounded by
superb illusionistic floral borders, place it
among the very finest of the manuscripts
produced in Flanders by the founders of
the Ghent/Bruges School, one of the last
great styles of illumination. Lord Hastings'
arms appear in the margin of the recto.

(Above) *Page 12*

THE VISITATION

BL Egerton MS 1070 f.29v. French,
early 15th century.
220 x 160 mm

THIS MANUSCRIPT was painted by one of
the leading Parisian illuminators of the
early 15th century. It later belonged to
René of Anjou, titular king of Naples and
Jerusalem, who died in 1480. His daughter
Margaret was married to King Henry VI of
England. The recto (page 13) contains an
image which has been replaced by text for
the purposes of this book.

(Above) *Pages 14 – 15*

THE NATIVITY

The Sforza Hours. BL Additional MS 34294 f.82v.
Italian, about 1490, with Flemish additions
made in 1519.
130 x 95 mm

THE ORIGINAL OWNER of the manuscript, illuminated
by the Milanese court painter Pietro Birago, was
Bona of Savoy (D 1503), the wife of Galeazzo Maria
Sforza, Duke of Milan. Unfinished at the time of her
death, the manuscript eventually passed into the hands
of Margaret of Austria who paid the Flemish miniaturist,
Gerard Horenbout, to provide the 16 miniatures,
including this Nativity, needed to complete the work
containing 64 miniatures in total. Horenbout took great
pains to copy the format and range of colouring which he
found in the book's Italian miniatures, but his landscapes
and the faces of his characters are typically Flemish.

(Left) *Pages 16 – 17*

The Annunciation to the Shepherds

The Bedford Hours. BL Additional MS
18850 f.70v. Paris, about 1423.
260 x 180 mm
(See entry for cover image)

Each of the main miniatures of the manuscript is accompanied by an elaborate set of marginal roundels. The marginal roundels decorating the text pages cover the whole of the New Testament, each episode accompanied either by its Old Testament prefiguration, or by some form of pictorial commentary. The reader's understanding is aided by explanatory 'subtitles' written at the bottom; on the text pages, they are written in blue and gold and on each main miniature page, in blue and red.

(Right) *Pages 18 – 19*

The Presentation in the Temple

Additional MS 31834 f.66.
Paris, second quarter of the 15th century.
245 x 175 mm

In this version of the Presentation, the Jewish priest is shown garbed as a Christian bishop. The manuscript is one of a number bequeathed to the national collection in 1881 by William Burges, the Victorian architect and designer, whose own work was heavily influenced by medieval models.

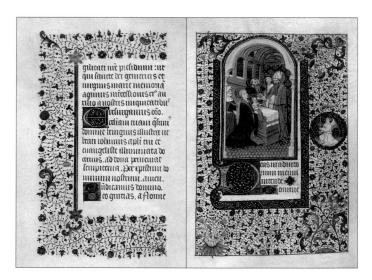

(Left) *Pages 20 – 21*

The Epiphany

Egerton MS 2125 f.182v.
Flemish, early 16th century.
155 x 100 mm

This elegant little book, containing 22 miniatures and borders of flowers, insects and jewels, was made in the workshop of the celebrated Flemish illuminator Simon Bening, apparently for the personal use of the abbess of Messines, near Ypres in West Flanders.

(Right) *Pages 22 – 23 and back cover*
(detail)

The Flight to Egypt

Additional MS 25695 f.114.
Paris, about 1470.
190 x 135 mm

The story of Joseph's dream is told on a scroll wound around the tree trunks that enclose the main miniature. Inside a bejewelled frame the Holy Family crosses the foreground. Behind them a farmer is interrogated by Herod's soldiers. The margins of the folio are peopled with figures depicting the story of the Massacre of the Innocents.

(Left) *Pages 24 – 25*

The Holy Family

Additional MS 18193 f.48v.
Spanish, second half of the 15th century.
195 x 135 mm

A special mass in honour of the Virgin is frequently found in Books of Hours. In this manuscript it begins with an illustration of the Holy Family in St Joseph's carpenter's shop. An array of tools hangs from the wall at the back of the picture, most of them very little different from those in use today. The Virgin is at work on some embroidery, her materials supported on a cushion and a work-basket at her side. The Child has toys and a bird in a cage. The entire scene could represent an episode in the contemporary everyday life.

A Medieval Christmas copyright © 1996 by Frances Lincoln Limited
Text copyright © 1996 by Yale University
Illustrations copyright © 1996 by The British Library Board

First published by
Frances Lincoln Limited, London, U.K.

First North American Edition

ISBN 0-8212-2279-1

Library of Congress Catalog Card Number 95-82125

Bulfinch Press is an imprint and trademark of Little, Brown and Company (Inc.)
Published simultaneously in Canada by Little, Brown & Company (Canada) Limited

PRINTED IN HONG KONG